BEARS

NORTH AMERICAN ANIMAL DISCOVERY LIBRARY

Lynn M. Stone

Rourke Corporation, Inc.
Vero Beach, Florida 32964

PHOTO CREDITS

All photos by author except: title page, pages 17, 18 © Tom
and Pat Leeson

LIBRARY OF CONGRESS
Library of Congress Cataloging-in-Publication Data
Stone, Lynn M., 1942-
 Bears / by Lynn M. Stone.

 p. cm. — (North American animal discovery library)
 Summary: An introduction to the physical characteristics,
habits, and natural environment, and future prospects of the
three species of bears that live in North america.
 ISBN 0-86593-042-2
 1. Bears—Juvenile literature. [1. Bears.] I. Title.
II. Series: Stone, Lynn M., 1942- North American animal
discovery library.
QL737.C27S76   1990
599.74'446—dc20   89-70168
                              CIP
                              AC

Bears

TABLE OF CONTENTS

THE BEAR

Bears are the largest meat-eating animals in North America. Some grizzly bears *(Ursus arctos)* are the largest meat-eating animals on land anywhere in the world!

Grizzly bears—sometimes called brown bears—of Kodiak Island, Alaska, weigh up to 1,700 pounds. The largest tigers and lions weigh no more than 700 pounds.

Three kinds, or **species,** of bears live in North America. They are the black *(Ursus americanus),* grizzly, and polar *(Ursus maritimus)* bears. Black bears weigh 200 to 600 pounds. Polar bears weigh 900 to 1,100 pounds.

Polar bear

THE BEAR'S COUSINS

The bears of North America have several bear cousins elsewhere. There are eight species of bears found throughout much of the world.

The brown bears of Europe and Asia are like the brown bears of North America. The Asiatic black bear is similar, also, to the American black bear.

The spectacled bear of South America doesn't have a close relative in North America.

The giant panda of China is often called a "panda bear." It is a distant cousin of the American bears.

Spectacled bear

HOW THEY LOOK

Bears are large, heavy-bodied animals with thick fur. Black bears are not always black. In the West they may be light brown or even blue-gray.

Brown bears—the grizzlies—are found in several shades of brown.

Polar bears, except for their noses and eyes, are white or cream-colored.

All bears have large paws with long claws.

Grizzlies are the heaviest and longest of the bears. A big Kodiak grizzly may measure 11 feet. Standing on its hind legs, it towers above a man.

Black bear

WHERE THEY LIVE

Bears of one kind or another live in most of North America. During much of the year, polar bears live on the ice of the frozen Arctic Ocean. They rarely travel very far onto land.

Grizzlies live mostly in the mountains of Alaska, western Canada, and the northern Rocky Mountains of the United States.

Black bears live in most of Canada and in much of the United States. They are found in forests, mountains and swamps.

Black bear in tree

Kodiak Island grizzly

Polar bear diving

HOW THEY LIVE

Bears have poor eyesight, but they have a fine sense of smell. Sometimes they sniff while standing on their hind feet.

Fat and fur protect bears from cold, but during the worst winter weather, black and grizzly bears sleep in their dens. Pregnant polar bears also sleep away the winter in a den.

Bears are surprisingly fast. A grizzly can run almost 40 miles per hour. No human can outrace a charging bear.

All bears can swim, but polar bears are excellent swimmers.

Black bear cub

THE BEAR'S CUBS

Baby bears are born in a den. They are about the size of squirrels.

Mother bears have **cubs** once every two years. The cubs usually stay with their mother until they are almost two. When the mother bear, called a **sow,** is ready to have more cubs, she chases her two-year olds away.

A sow has from one to four cubs. Usually she has twins.

Wild bears normally live from 15 to 30 years. One captive grizzly lived to be 47 years old.

Grizzly sow with cubs

PREDATOR AND PREY

Bears are usually the most powerful **predators,** or hunters, wherever they live. Bears often catch animals for their food. But bears like plants too.

The black bear eats twigs, leaves, nuts, corn, and berries along with small animals, fish, and deer.

Grizzlies kill many large animals, such as mountain goats and elk. They also eat mice, marmots, salmon, roots, and berries.

Polar bears live only on meat when they are on the Arctic ice. Their **prey**—the animals that they kill—includes walrus, seals, and fish.

Grizzly eating berries

BEARS AND PEOPLE

Indians used bear skins for warmth and bear claws for jewelry. They often ate bear meat.

In the Far North, **Inuit** people also hunted bears for their fur and meat.

Hunters still shoot black bears in many states and Canadian provinces. Grizzly bears are hunted in a few places.

Bears can be trained to perform. They are often shown in circuses and wild animal shows.

Bears can be extremely dangerous if they are scared or if they have cubs.

Polar bears

THE BEAR'S FUTURE

Black bears are still fairly common in many places. **Endangered** animals are in danger of becoming **extinct,** or disappearing forever.

The grizzly is endangered over much of its range. Ranchers have killed large numbers of grizzlies, because the bears were seen as a threat to sheep and cattle.

Polar bears were hunted for many years, and these great white bears became scarce. Polar bears are protected now by all the countries of the Far North. The polar bear's future seems fairly safe.

Glossary

cubs (CUBS)—baby bears

endangered (en DANE jerd)—in danger of no longer existing; very rare

extinct (ex TINKT)—no longer existing

Inuit (IN u it)—one group of native people in the North American Arctic; Eskimos

predator (PRED a tor)—an animal that kills other animals for food

prey (PREY)—an animal that is hunted by another for food

species (SPEE sheez)—within a group of closely related animals, one certain kind, such as a black bear

sow (SOU)—a female bear

INDEX